California & the Pacific Coast Highway Travel Guide

Attractions, Eating, Drinking, Shopping & Places To Stay

Oliver Bell

Copyright © 2014, Astute Press
All Rights Reserved.

No part of this publication may be reproduced, stored in a retrieval system, or transmitted, in any form or by any means without the prior written permission of the publisher, nor be otherwise circulated in any form of binding or cover other than that in which it is published and without similar condition being imposed on the subsequent purchaser.

If there are any errors or omissions in copyright acknowledgements the publisher will be pleased to insert the appropriate acknowledgement in any subsequent printing of this publication.

Although we have taken all reasonable care in researching this book we make no warranty about the accuracy or completeness of its content and disclaim all liability arising from its use

Table of Contents

California 8
Culture 10
Location & Orientation 11
Climate & When to Visit 11

Sightseeing Highlights 13
Hollywood 13
Long Beach 15
Los Angeles 17
Napa Valley 18
Sacramento 19
San Diego 21
San Francisco 22
Santa Monica 23
Sonoma 24
Yosemite Valley 26

Recommendations for the Budget Traveler 28
Places to Stay 28
Adelaide Hostel (San Francisco) 28
San Francisco City Center Hostel 29
USA Hostels San Diego 30
Venice Beach Cotel 31
Yosemite Bug Rustic Mountain Resort 32
Places to Eat & Drink 33
Café La Boheme 33
Chaya Downtown 34
In-N-Out Burger 35
The Red Grape 35
Thomas Keller Restaurant Group 36
Ad Hoc 36
Bouchon Bakery Beverly Hills 37
Bouchon Bakery Yountville 37
Bouchon Bistro Yountville 37
French Laundry 38
Places to Shop 39
Abbot Kinney Boulevard 39

  Fillmore Street 40
  Santee Alley 41
  Skeletons in the Closet 42
  Third Street Promenade 43
Pacific Coast Highway..**44**
 Culture **46**
 Location & Orientation..**47**
 Climate & When to Visit **47**
Sightseeing Highlights..**48**
 Santa Barbara...**48**
  Old Mission Santa Barbara..48
  Karpeles Manuscript Library Museum 49
  Rattlesnake Canyon 50
  Chumash Painted Cave State Historic Park 51
  Stearns Wharf..52
  Santa Barbara Museum of Art 52
  Santa Barbara Zoo 53
 Solvang & Santa Ynez Valley...**54**
  Santa Ynez Valley Visitors Association 54
  Elverhoj Museum of History & Art 55
  Hans Christian Andersen Museum 55
  Solvang Vintage Motorcycle Museum 56
  Old Mission Santa Ines...57
 San Luis Obispo..**57**
  San Luis Obispo Convention Bureau 57
  Hearst Castle 58
 Big Sur..**59**
  Bixby Bridge 59
 Carmel..**60**
  Point Lobos State Reserve Park..60
  San Carlos Borromeo de Carmelo Mission 61
 Monterey..**62**
  Cannery Row...62
  Monterey Bay Aquarium..62
  Pebble Beach Golf Links 63
  17-Mile Drive 64
Recommendations for the Budget Traveler **65**
 Places to Stay..**65**
  Santa Barbara 65
  Hotel Oceana Santa Barbara..65

    Inn at East Beach 66
    Solvang 66
    Wine Valley Inn 66
    King Frederik Inn 67
    San Luis Obispo 68
    Vagabond Inn, San Luis Obispo 68
    La Cuesta Inn 68
    Big Sur 69
    Ripplewood Resort 69
    Davenport Roadhouse 69
    Carmel 70
    Carmel Mission Inn 70
    Carmel River Inn 70
    Monterey 71
    Cannery Row Inn 71
    Casa Munras 72
Places to Eat **72**
    Santa Barbara 72
    The Brewhouse Santa Barbara 72
    Taqueria El Bajio 73
    Solvang 73
    Belgian Café 73
    Viking Garden Restaurant 74
    San Luis Obispo 74
    Franks Famous Hot Dogs 74
    Chino's Rock & Tacos 75
    Big Sur 75
    Nepenthe Restaurant 75
    Rocky Point Restaurant 76
    Carmel 76
    Bahama Island Steakhouse 76
    Earthbound Farm 77
    Monterey 77
    Sly McFly's 77
    Papa Chevo's Taco Shop 78
Places to Shop **78**
    Santa Barbara 78
    Santa Barbara Farmer's Market 78
    Paseo Nuevo Shopping Center 79
    Solvang & Santa Ynez Valley 79
    Ingeborg's 79

Windmill Glassworks	80
San Luis Obispo	80
Apple Farm Gift Shop & Millhouse	80
Kwirkworld	81
Big Sur	81
Local Color	81
Big Sur Bizarre	82
Carmel	82
Carmel Bay Company	82
The Barnyard Shopping Village	83
Monterey	83
Ghirardelli Chocolate & Ice Cream Shop	83
The Wharf's General Store	84

California

California, known as the Golden State, is the third largest and most populous state in the United States. With a diverse history encompassing the former territory of Mexico, the gold rush, and leadership in the movie, music, tourism and hi-tech industries, California has its major cities of Los Angeles, San Francisco, San Jose/Silicon Valley and San Diego but much more.

California's capital, Sacramento, is the 35th largest city in the United States. California began as a Spanish territory before being sold to Mexico. After the fight for independence, California joined the Union as the 31st state in 1850. Its motto, "Eureka," is indicative of the state's passion for discovery, independence, and progression. California's cities as well as Hollywood are known for their close proximity to many celebrities of hi-tech (e.g. Steve Jobs), movies (e.g. Tom Cruise) and sports (e.g. David Beckham).

Silicon Valley is located in Northern California near to Stanford University and is home to some of the largest technology and Internet companies in the world including Apple, Google and Facebook.

The culinary field is also continually evolving in California and allows vegan and animal rights activists the opportunity to express their issues with certain celebrity chefs and their preparation techniques and food choices. For example, Foie Gras (goose liver) was banned from production in 2012. Many food movements originated in California and some remarkable restaurants are located in Napa Valley, San Francisco, Los Angeles, Berkeley and almost everywhere else.

Culture

Due to its proximity to Mexico and its history, a large part of California's culture has a Hispanic background. With almost 30% of the population speaking Spanish as a first or second language and a large amount of migrant workers, the Hispanic culture is prevalent throughout the state, particularly in Southern California.

California is also strongly influenced by various Asian influences due to the ease of immigration across the Pacific Ocean. The Chinese first arrived in the 1850s with the Japanese following suit in the 1880s and a large influx of many Southeast Asians after the Vietnam War ended in the 1970s. The Chinese and Japanese greatly assisted with California's early commercial and economic development. Cupertino, home to Apple, has one of the largest expat Taiwanese communities in the world.

Many of the larger cities in California are home to prevalent Lesbian, Gay, Bisexual, and Transgender (LGBT) communities. These cities, in particular San Francisco, are known for their liberal stances on many social issues.

There are many professional sports teams across the state that allows residents and visitors to proudly proclaim their loyalties on an almost daily basis.

Location & Orientation

California is the westernmost state in the continental United States. Its location along the Pacific Ring of Fire contributes to its more than 35,000 earthquakes per year (almost all of them being "minor"). It is bordered on the west by the Pacific Ocean. The southern border is part of the Baja Peninsula of Mexico. Oregon is to the immediate north with Nevada and Arizona to the east. Due to its area of 160,000 square miles, California has a diverse array of geographical regions. The Central Valley is one of the top agricultural areas in the United States. Mount Whitney, in the Sierra Nevada, is the highest peak in the continental United States with an elevation of 14,505 feet. Death Valley, located in the Mojave Desert (Southern California), is the lowest point at 282 feet below sea level.

Climate & When to Visit

Most of the state experiences a Mediterranean climate with mild winters and dry summers, making this a favorite tourist destination throughout the year. The Sierra Nevada (Yosemite/Lake Tahoe area) has an alpine climate with snow in the winter and mild summers. The Mojave Desert is hot and dry throughout the year, thus inspiring the name "Death Valley."

In the Central Valley (Fresno, Stockton etc.), temperatures are mild throughout the year, yielding ideal weather for agriculture. The temperatures along the coast and valleys are mostly mild, but vary along each area. This gives visitors a different time to visit for each area. San Francisco experiences an average high of 72 degrees in July and August, while Walnut Creek averages 90 degrees during the same months and is only 20 miles inward. Silicon Valley, located about 50 miles to the south of San Francisco, has a climate that's on average warmer than San Francisco but cooler than Walnut Creek.

Due to its location between the ocean and mountain ranges, some parts of California experience heavy rainfall throughout the year. The Coast Redwood forest can receive up to 100 inches of rainfall per year with Northwestern California receiving anywhere between 15 inches and 50 inches of precipitation. East of the Rocky Mountains is much drier, contributing to the desert climate in the Sierra Nevada and Peninsular Ranges.

In addition to its climatatic disparities, California can be victim to a number of natural disasters, including earthquakes, forest fires, and tropical storms. Forest fires are more likely in the spring and fall due to Santa Ana winds blowing towards Southern California from the eastern mountains. The dryness makes the potential for forest fires more likely.

Sightseeing Highlights

Hollywood

This famous district of Los Angeles is known as the epicenter of the entertainment industry. Due to its location in one of the largest states in the U.S. and its concentration of actors, directors, and others in the entertainment business, it is a favorite for tourists looking to see the rich and famous.

Hollywood is so well known across the world that other regions' film industries have based their names on it, including Bollywood in India and Nollywood in Nigeria. Visitors can also tour the Santa Clarita and San Fernando valleys to see other portions of the movie industry, but most of the editing, special effects, lighting and pre/post-production portions of movie making are completed in the Hollywood area.

Paramount Pictures, one of the major film companies still in existence, is located in Hollywood, as well as other, smaller studios. Academy Award fans can stop by the Doly Theatre, more famously known as the Kodak Theatre, to visit the site of the annual Oscar Award Ceremony.

The Hollywood Walk of Fame is a 15-block sidewalk, with more than 2,400 terrazzo and brass stars, designed to recognize those with great contributions to the entertainment history. Actors, directors, musicians and theatrical groups, and even fictional characters are represented. In addition to the honoree's name, a round emblem is inlaid indicating the person or group's contribution. One of five emblems can be chosen, honoring the person's contribution in motion pictures, broadcast radio, audio recording or music, broadcast television, or live performances. Sponsors and corporations are also incorporated, but with unique badges.

Grauman's Theatre, an instantly recognizable stop on the Hollywood Walk of Fame, is the location for the handprint and footprint ceremonies that many well-known stars participate in. Since 1927, over 200 actors, actresses, and directors have placed their hand and footprints in wet concrete outside of the theater. This is now popular as a spot for visitors to place their own hands in the indentations. It is also the location for many movie premieres, attracting numerous celebrities and countless fans along the red carpet.

The Hollywood Bowl is the largest natural amphitheater in the U.S. It seats almost 18,000 people and is used primarily for musical performances (take a picnic to eat in the grounds before hand). The Hollywood sign in the Hills can be seen in the background. Festivals and symphonies are held each year and the site has featured countless remarkable shows since its inception in 1922. Depending on the headliner, tickets can be expensive, but the Bowl is a must-see during a trip to Hollywood.

Long Beach

Long Beach is located in the Greater Los Angeles area. It can be found approximately 20 miles south of downtown Los Angeles. Its port is one of the largest shipping ports in the world as well as the second-busiest container port. Many well-defined neighborhoods are situated in Long Beach with their own personalities and advocacy groups.

Ship enthusiasts will enjoy visiting the RMS Queen Mary, an art deco ocean liner from 1963. It was the fastest liner for almost 15 years and is now a museum. The Aquarium of the Pacific is a favorite among visitors, housing over 12,500 species, including an area to pet sharks.

In the canals of Naples, riders can experience romantic singing gondolier trips. The East Village Arts District is home to multiple art galleries and shops and hosts a monthly Artwalk every second Saturday. Lesser-known artists are able to display their pieces for sale, allowing visitors to pick up unique art for their homes and businesses.

Depending on what time of year you visit Southern California, you may want to buy tickets to one of the many music festivals in Long Beach. The Bob Marley Reggae Festival is held each February. Every September features a blues festival and there is a Brazilian Street Carnaval. If you like salsa or Hawaiian music and are taking a trip in June, the El Dia De San Juan Puerto Rican festival and Aloha Concert Jam are held, respectively. Symphony and Opera performances also performed throughout the year.

Holiday season visitors may experience a Christmas boat parade, with one held each weekend from December 1 through December 25. If you're looking to encounter the LGBT movement while in Southern California, the Long Beach Lesbian and Gay Pride Parade and Festival is held each summer. As with many areas in California, Long Beach has a long and varied history of cultural attractions.

Los Angeles

The most populous city in California, Los Angeles is also the name of the most ethnically diverse county in the United States. Some of the landmarks in Los Angeles are located in Hollywood and Long Beach, due to its classification as a metropolis. Los Angeles has something for everybody, whether visitors are looking for celebrity homes, wineries, religious buildings, beaches or cultural attractions, among others.

People of all backgrounds will enjoy Disneyland. The park and resort in Anaheim is owned and operated by the Walt Disney Company. It has the Disney California Adventure Park to honor its home state's culture and extensive history. Additionally, the theme park and entertainment district is composed of attractions for all types, with restaurants, shops, and spas in addition to its rides and eight "lands," which are its themed areas of the resort.

Disneyland is recommended for a full-day visit, due to its expansive size and number of sites to visit. If you're worried about walking the vastness of the park, there is not only a train, but also a monorail system and various vehicles along Main Street. Live shows are held throughout the day and each night, so plan the trip accordingly.

Sports fans will also want to view the famous Dodger Stadium and Staples Center to see where their favorite teams play. The Staples Center hosts performance arts events and shows throughout the year in addition to its multiple sports games.

Those interested in architecture and modern buildings will want to see the iconic Theme Building at the Los Angeles International Airport (LAX). The structure looks like a flying saucer on four legs and cost $4 million and $12.3 million to renovate in 1997 and 2010, respectively. The Encounter Restaurant is located directly below the Observation Level and offers its diners an opportunity to see the view across Los Angeles.

Napa Valley

One of the nine San Francisco Bay Area counties, Napa County is known primarily for its vineyards and restaurants, located in and around Napa Valley. Some of the world's best wines are produced in Napa Valley with more than four hundred wineries and multiple grape varieties.
It is the center of the US wine industry and located about 30 miles northeast of San Francisco.

Every June, the Napa Valley Wine Auction is held. Wines and other prizes from the area's wineries are auctioned off to the highest bidder. Several charities in the county receive the portions of the event's proceeds.
If you're visiting in mid-July, it may coincide with the valley's annual music, food, wine, and art festival. Festival del Sole is a relatively new festival, and attracts thousands of people each year to take pleasure in the various items for sale in addition to various performances. Tickets are available with various options. Be aware that tickets start at $500 and can reach up to $7,500 or more!

Outdoors enthusiasts can take in the beautiful scenery for little to no cost. Many trails allow dogs, but visitors should check the schedule because some trails are closed during the winter. The Mount St. Helena Trail includes landmarks, such as the Robert Louis Stevenson memorial and Bubble Rock for climbers. The gorgeous surroundings of Napa Valley make for a wonderful, picturesque trip to Northern California.

Sacramento

The capital of California, Sacramento is also the sixth largest city in California. It has multiple cultural attractions, particularly in the music, theater, and history industries. One unique festival held each year is the Trash Film Orgy, devoted to celebrating horror, monster, exploitative, absurd B-movies. From mid-June through mid-August, the Trash Film Orgy kicks off with a zombie walk and shows trash movies on the big screen throughout the summer. Costumes are encouraged.

Along the same vein, the Sacramento Horror Film Festival showcases live performances and feature-length and short films in the horror and macabre genres. A Zombie Beauty Pageant kicks off the festival, followed by the Rocky Horror Picture Show before programs are held throughout the weekend.

Sacramento residents celebrate other film genres, also hosting separate French and Japanese Film Festivals each July. Fans of classical literature may want to plan their visit in the summer to attend the Sacramento Shakespeare Festival in William Land Park.

Interested in tasting some of the fine restaurants located in Sacramento? Guy Fieri from the Food Network has a fusion restaurant entitled Tex Wasabi. Café Rolle offers Sacramento authentic French food. Those craving Italian should visit Biba Restaurant with the choice of either à la carte dishes or prix fix menus from Monday through Wednesday.

In addition to its cultural attractions, Sacramento is also host to amusement parks, casinos, and the Jelly Belly Candy Company. The factory offers free 40-minute tours every day between 9 am – 4 pm. One of the historic monuments is the California Vietnam Veterans Memorial, located on the State Capitol grounds. 5,822 names are engraved on 22 black granite panels, listing all of California's dead or missing after the Vietnam War was ended. Five bronze statues depict scenes of daily life while in Vietnam.

Be aware that temperatures in Sacramento can be particularly high in summer. Many consecutive days with highs above 100 F are not uncommon. Humidity is typically low however.

San Diego

For a beach-centered vacation, visitors will want to stop by San Diego. With extensive beaches along the coast of the Pacific Ocean as well as bordering Mexico, San Diego is a favorite year-round destination due to its lovely climate.

One of the most well known sites in the city is its famous San Diego Zoo. Located in Balboa Park, the zoo is home to more than 3,700 animals, including the giant pandas. The zoo and safari park concurrently operate as an arboretum with its rare plant collection. Both eucalyptus trees and bamboo trees are harvested for its koalas and pandas, respectively. The climate of San Diego is well suited for the animals that originate from rainforests.

The LGBT Pride Parade and Festival is held each July in the San Diego Hillcrest neighborhood. There are also seasonal festivals held throughout the year for holidays and communities. Restaurant Week is held bi-annually in January and September.

The internationally renowned Comic-Con is also held every summer in San Diego. Although there are variations in cities across the United States, the original Comic-Con draws thousands of science fiction celebrities and their fans.

Every October, San Diego hosts its "Fall for the Arts" for National Arts and Humanities Month. Multiple all-ages festivals are held throughout the month. The San Diego Beer Week is held each November to celebrate craft beers with various pairings and activities for guests 21 and up. Tickets vary from $10 to $55, depending on the type of ticket bought.

San Francisco

San Francisco has a variety of sites that attract tourists from across the world. In addition to its architectural gems, the city has many distinct neighborhoods with their own unique character.

San Francisco's Chinatown neighborhood is the oldest Chinatown in the country. It rivals New York's Chinatown in importance and has many restaurants, shops, and attractions on offer. The Haight-Ashbury neighborhood was once associated with the hippie culture of the 1960s, but is now filled with expensive boutiques and a few chain stores while retaining its bohemian atmosphere.

San Francisco is also known for its large LGBT population and hosts one of the largest Pride Parades in the country. Every June, San Francisco hosts the LGBT Pride Celebration at the foot of City Hall, in memoriam of former gay-advocate, Harvey Milk who was murdered in city hall in the late-seventies.

Another favorite spot for the LGBT community and supporters is Dolores Park, otherwise known as "The Gay Beach." It always has a large collection of young people and is the place to see and be seen. The Castro district of San Francisco is the most famous gay neighborhood in the country.

Don't miss the Golden Gate Bridge (and the Golden Gate National Park). The bridge has been in existence for over 75 years and is one of the most visited landmarks in the United States. The trademark red color of the bridge makes for a fantastic photo opportunity with many viewpoints available on both sides of the bridge. The art deco style meshes perfectly with the culture of San Francisco and its surrounding areas.

Santa Monica

Another popular destination for beach lovers is Santa Monica. Situated on the Santa Monica Bay in western Los Angeles County, this city is a popular residence for many celebrities and wealthy executives. Students, surfers, and young professionals are represented among its many single-family, affluent neighborhoods.

The Santa Monica Pier houses the Santa Monica Loof Hippodrome – a carousel – as well as an aquarium, cafés, shops, a trapeze school, and the La Monica Ballroom. The carousel is a recognizable spot on the city's skyline.

If you're interested in other outdoor activities in addition to the famous beach, the Santa Monica Steps go from north of San Vicente into Santa Monica Canyon. The steps are quite a workout and attract people from surrounding areas as well as tourists looking to work off some of the delicious food found in the local restaurants.

Santa Monica is known for its skateboarding culture and there are many events held throughout the year here. The Santa Monica Chamber of Commerce holds the Taste of Santa Monica each Fall. Guests can sample food and drinks from local restaurants while enjoying the view from the Santa Monica Pier.

Sonoma

Sonoma is the other major part of California's Wine Country region and is located in Sonoma Valley. Considered the birthplace of California wine making, Sonoma also hosts the Valley of the Moon Vintage Festival in late-September. The Zinfandel/Primitivo grape varietal was first introduced in Sonoma.

Literature fans will be interested in the Jack London State Historic Park, positioned along the eastern slope of Sonoma Mountain. Jack London and his wife are buried on their former property, now a National Historic Landmark.

If you're interested in experiencing the more temperate climates of California during the colder winters elsewhere, Sonoma Valley holds an Olive Festival every December through February. Blessings, tastings, and other events are also held at wineries and other facilities each month.

Visitors can also stop by the olive trees in the Sonoma State Historic Park for a small fee: Adults pay $3, children 6-17 pay $2, and children under 6 are free. The festival culminates in seminars, artisan markets, concerts, and other olive-themed events that are fun for the whole family.

Film buffs can find film festivals across the world but Sonoma Valley hosts its Sonoma International Film Festival every April. Combining film, food, and wine, it incorporates student films from the local high school along with professionally made films to showcase over 100 films each festival.

Visitors interested in wine tastings can stop by the oldest commercial winery in California: the Buena Vista Winery. Founded in 1857, it now produces 500,000 cases of wine and the vineyard spans over 900 acres. The winery produces all types of wine to satiate all types of wine drinkers, including syrah, pinot noir, chardonnay, cabernet sauvignon, and merlot.

Finally, one of the newer festivals is held each Labor Day Weekend. The Sonoma Wine Country Weekend donates its proceeds to area non-profits and coincides with the Sonoma Valley Harvest Wine Auction. Held at many of the vineyards across the Valley, the weekend is another chance for the restaurants and wineries to showcase their products during dinner parties, barbecues, and lunches, in addition to the tastings they hold throughout the year.

Yosemite Valley

The Yosemite Valley is one of the reasons why Yosemite National Park is so breathtaking and well preserved. The glacial valley is located in the western Sierra Nevada Mountains close to Nevada and is located about 2-3 hours drive of the San Francisco region.

The stunning waterfalls are best to visit in the spring, as the snow is melting and before they dry up by late summer. Hikers can trek across the valley to view El Capitan, Cathedral Rocks, and the Sentinel Meadow. Cross the Sentinel Bridge to view the Merced River and Half Dome from afar. Much can be seen from a simple drive through the valley as well.

There are various hiking paths depending on the strength and experience of the hikers. Park rangers and staffers in Yosemite National Park distribute various guides.

Rock climbing enthusiasts will also enjoy a visit to Yosemite Valley to meet with other climbers while attempting to reach the granite summits. El Capitan, Cathedral Rocks, Three Brothers, and Half Dome are the primary rockfaces that are scaled by climbers.

A beautiful, spectacularly natural area, memories of Yosemite Valley will stay with visitors for many years to come.

Recommendations for the Budget Traveler

Places to Stay

Adelaide Hostel (San Francisco)

5 Isadora Duncan Lane
San Francisco, California, 94102
http://www.adelaidehostel.com/

This charming hostel, found in the former Adelaide Inn and Hotel, is in downtown San Francisco, less than two blocks from Union Square.

There are private rooms in addition to dorm-style rooms. The private single and double rooms start at $60, although the three and four person private rooms begin at $26. Dorm rooms can be either single sex or co-ed and start at $23 per person each day. Breakfast is included in the rates in addition to free linens, wireless Internet, and free safes. Nearby sites to see are Alcatraz, Chinatown, Fisherman's Wharf and Haight Ashbury – a former rock and roll haven.

San Francisco City Center Hostel

685 Ellis Street
San Francisco, CA, 94109
(415) 474-5271
http://www.sfhostels.com/city-center/

This hostel, located in the former Atherton Hotel, was recently renovated and offers private and dorm-style rooms, with private bathrooms per room. Linens, continental breakfast, WiFi, and other activities are included as well as an in-house café and low-cost services. Guests can walk to the Civic Center arts district and experience the gastronomical fare and nightlife.

Cultural attractions, such as the San Francisco Opera, Symphony, and Ballet, are located nearby. The dorm rates are quite affordable, starting at only $28. Private rooms begin at $89. However, the rates vary based on the season, so check prior to making travel plans. Group rates are also available and Hostelling International members receive discounts on their rooms. When you arrive, check with staff to see what activities and events will be held. They can give you a list of some free or low-cost attractions in addition to what the hostel has available.

USA Hostels San Diego

726 5th Avenue
San Diego, California 92101
619-232-3100
http://www.usahostels.com/sandiego/

This hostel in San Diego is owned by one of the highest rated hostel companies in the world. It is located in the Gaslamp District and offers competitive rates and amenities that make it one of the best bargains in the city. Linens, coffee, tea, and pancakes are included in the room rates. Due to its proximity to the San Diego Zoo, museums, and the Harbor, the hostel can provide discounted entrance tickets to guests.

Looking to get active while touring the city? Rent a discounted bike and check out the nearby Balboa Park and Harbor. Check the activity schedule, because the staff leads a pub-crawl each Wednesday and a weekly $19 trip to Tijuana on Saturdays, including transportation. Tequila tastings, margarita madness, and souvenir haggling are all found on these group tours. The dorm rooms also have "privacy pods" to help dissipate the noise and light for those looking for quiet time. Room rates start at $25 per person per night in the dorm rooms and increase based on size and type of room booked. However, rates can change depending on the season and local festivals or events. Check the website and call for questions and to book.

Venice Beach Cotel

25 Windward Avenue
Venice, California, 90291
310-496-1210
http://venicebeachcotel.com

If you're looking to hang ten with surfers and other young beach-lovers, then the Venice Beach Hostel is the perfect place. With colorfully painted murals on all the bedroom walls and the option of single-sex or mixed dorm rooms, in addition to the private rooms, this hostel exudes youth and fun. Breakfast is included with the stay and all those booking a private room must stay at least two nights.

There is an active nightlife nearby and in the hostel. A cleaning service comes once a day to clean all the rooms and there are free linens included in the room fees. Safes are available and security guards keep the area secure throughout the day and night. Everyone must bring their passport to check in, even American citizens.

Yosemite Bug Rustic Mountain Resort

6979 Highway 140
Midpines, California 95345
http://www.yosemitebug.com/

This unique resort is affordable and away from the hustle and bustle of city life. It is a great spot for folks who enjoy the outdoors and want to stay near Yosemite Valley while touring California. There are multiple options to choose from, whether guests are traveling alone, as a couple, or as a group. There are single sex and co-ed dormitories available, starting at $25 ($22 for Hostelling International members). Private rooms are also offered with the choice of either a private or shared bath. Private baths start at $75 and shared baths begin at $45.

For an experience different from other hostel visitors, Yosemite Bug has tent cabins with camping style restrooms and showers. There are 12 uninsulated and four insulated tent cabins with either twin beds or full beds inside. If you're traveling in a large group, a guesthouse may be a great option. The Barn Studio fits two to four people and costs between $155 and $195 per night.

The Starlite House can fit up to nine people and can cost up to $285. The house has two bedrooms downstairs, separate room connected to the house, and a day bed on the enclosed porch. The BBQ and deck outside make this a great getaway for friends or family who are looking to spend time together and enjoy the outdoors.

Yosemite Bug is environmentally friendly and has a café that serves three meals a day, with a guest kitchen also available. The Health Spa offers a $10 day pass for luxuries, such as a hot tub, sauna, many amenities and services. Caught the travel bug? Feed it with a stay in Yosemite Bug Rustic Mountain Resort.

Places to Eat & Drink

Café La Boheme

8400 Santa Monica Blvd
West Hollywood, California, 90069
323-848-2360
http://www.cafelaboheme.us/en/sas/welcome/top/

This quirky little café is located across the street from an Oriental rug shop and next door to a beauty supply store. Down the street is a tattoo shop and pizzeria.

However, don't let the neighborhood fool you. The charming building offers a variety of food and, during the daily happy hours from 5:00 – 7:30 p.m. PST, diners get half off all fun bites and sandwiches. You can stop by and munch on Filet Mignon Sliders for only $7.50 or get an order of steamed mussels for $8.50. Looking for international fare? Café La Boheme also offers chicken kara age – a Japanese style fried chicken – for only $5. If you're just looking for something to munch on during pre-dinner drinks, the shoestring fries will only cost you $3 during Happy Hour. Feel free to stay for dinner, however, for fresh dishes from the sea, meats, pasta, and vegetarian options.

Chaya Downtown

525 S. Flower St
Los Angeles, California, 90071
213-236-9577
www.thechaya.com/downtown-la/

Another good Happy Hour spot with affordable drinks and eats is Chaya. A Japanese restaurant that has locations across California and in Tokyo, Chaya has a wonderful happy hour from 4:00 p.m. to close on Monday through Friday and 5:00 p.m. to close on Saturday and Sunday.

The happy hour plates start at $5 with the mainstays of hummus and sweet potato fries. However, you can get steamed mussels or grilled octopus for only $8, if you're feeling adventurous. They also have an extensive sushi and sashimi list with an inside out albacore roll costing $5. The downtown signature rolls are more expensive, but diners can easily get their fill with cheap, yet quality choices.

In-N-Out Burger

http://www.in-n-out.com/

This burger chain is an example of uniquely Californian fast food. Although it is spreading eastward, its origins lie in California and the chain restaurants can be found up and down the Pacific Coast. The simple menu begets hesitation to the quality. However, the burgers, fries, and shakes are often highly-rated by native West Coasters. A trip to California will not be complete without at least one trip to an In-N-Out Burger, just to taste experience what all the hype is about.

The Red Grape

529 First Street West, Sonoma, CA 95476
707-996-4103
http://theredgrape.com/

Sometimes after a long day of wine tasting, you just want to take a nap or eat a cheap, hearty meal.

The Red Grape can't satisfy the nap portion, but with affordable prices for their dishes, it can satiate the latter. The pizza menu is split between red and white sauces and offers 20 different thin crust pizzas for less than $15. Get a classic Margherita pizza for only $13.25 or continue the wine-tasting theme with the Tuscan Sun pizza, also for $13.25, with ingredients such as roasted garlic, sun-dried tomatoes, and artichoke hearts.

Each month, The Red Grape offers different specials; so make sure to check them out before ordering. Did you buy any wine while touring the vineyards? If so, feel free to bring it to enjoy with your food. The restaurant only charges a $10 corkage fee, further cutting down on additional dinner costs. While enjoying its location in the beautiful Sonoma Valley, the Red Grape utilizes local ingredients and restaurants for its meat, pasta, produce, and bakery selections. This little restaurant owned by Carol and Sam Morphy is a wonderful experience without breaking the bank.

Thomas Keller Restaurant Group

http://tkrg.org/index.php

Ad Hoc

6476 Washington Street
Yountville, CA 94599
707-944-2487
http://www.adhocrestaurant.com/

Bouchon Bakery Beverly Hills

235 North Canon Drive
Beverly Hills, CA 90210
310-271-9910, ext. 621
http://bouchonbakery.com/beverly-hills

Bouchon Bakery Yountville

6528 Washington Street
Yountville, CA 94599
707-944-2253
http://bouchonbakery.com/yountville

Bouchon Bistro Yountville

6534 Washington Street
Yountville, CA 94599
707-944-8037
http://bouchonbistro.com/yountville

French Laundry

6640 Washington Street, Yountville, CA 94599
707-753-0088
http://www.frenchlaundry.com/

Opening his first restaurant in Yountville, California, Thomas Keller now owns five separate restaurants in Yountville and New York City. Bouchon Bakery is located in California, New York City, and Las Vegas.

Admittedly, all restaurants are a major splurge with the trademark prix fix menus. French Laundry and Per Se (in New York) both offer nine-course tasting menus. Each dish is a tiny, exquisite course to leave the diners wanting more. The French Laundry starts its tasting menus at $270 and reservations must be made months in advance. Ad Hoc is a newer restaurant that serves four-course dinners from Thursday through Tuesday. The prix fix meals start at $52 per person.

Bouchon Bistro is a bit more relaxed with a la carte menu items, specializing in *Fruits de Mer*, or fruits of the sea. The salads, sides, and appetizers are moderately priced. Mussels start at $7 per dozen and a seafood tasting option at $110. Caviar and French fries are also available, although it is suggested to eat them separately. All Thomas Keller restaurants focus on the highest quality and exquisitely made food.

His notoriety and reviews make the high prices for the tasting menus. However, if you want to try something on a Thomas Keller-approved menu without sacrificing a car payment, stop by the Bouchon Bakery in Yountville or Beverly Hills. The French baked goods are consistently top-rated. Enjoy the champagne lifestyle on a beer budget.

Places to Shop

Abbot Kinney Boulevard

Los Angeles, California, 90291
http://akinneycourt.com

Abbot Kinney Boulevard is a hip shopping center with an underground vibe. Its multiple independent shops and boutiques offer unique items that could either look great on your or on your wall. Repurposed signs and other items become tables, chairs, and jewelry at Altered Space Cowboy. All things surf, sand, and California are available at Surfing Cowboys, as well as some Native American-inspired textiles and tapestries.

The Get Activated Shop is a unique store partnering with Get Fit America. In order to acquire any drinks from the pop-up shop, visitors must earn them by exercising in a certain way, whether it be riding a stationary bike for 60 seconds, dancing freestyle for one minute, or lifting a year's worth of Activate drinks. The quirky shopping center offers dozens of stores and restaurants. A Taste of Abbot Kinney is held each October to support local artists. Other events and celebrations are held periodically to celebrate local bands, shops, and artists. The Intecollectuals – a sketch comedy troop – plays monthly at the Electric Lodge Theater. Check the website before you go to see what sales and specials are being held.

Fillmore Street

San Francisco, California 94115
http://www.fillmorestreetsf.com/

Fillmore Street is a uniquely affordable and fashionable haven for shoppers. In addition to its multiple boutiques, art galleries, and shoe stores, Fillmore Street is also home to florists, restaurants, and fitness clubs, among others. Located in the Fillmore District between Japantown and Pacific Heights, Fillmore Street is one of the best areas to visit on the West Coast for the up and coming trends and forever-classic pieces. There is even a jazz festival held annually in July, although jazz artists can be heard year-round in one of many jazz clubs in the district. Join the locals for a day.

Santee Alley

Los Angeles, California 90015
http://www.thesanteealley.com/

Located in the LA Fashion District, Santee Alley is a festive area to shop and find great bargains on quality goods. Visitors can find it in downtown Los Angeles between East 12th Street, Santee Street, Maple Avenue, and Olympic Boulevard.

There are more than 150 shops in Santee Alley that cover a variety of categories, including apparel, accessories, shoes, cosmetics, perfumes, and other gifts. These are primarily local or California-only shops. The number of choices can be overwhelming, in addition to the small size of the shops and amount of items located inside. However, the bargains are not to be missed, nor the opportunity to haggle prices.

Skeletons in the Closet

1104 N Mission Road
Los Angeles, CA 90033
323-343-0760
http://www.lacoroner.com/

This fun store offers many kitschy souvenir items, but with a deadly sense of humor. Every item for sale displays a design that is significant for the Los Angeles County Coroner, such as a skeleton, chalked-out body outline, or LA County Coroner seal. Various types of apparel for the body are sold at moderate prices for souvenirs. Office supplies, home décor, and more can either add the perfect touch to a murder mystery party or spook your neighbors in the office. At the very least, this shop is one to check out while in Los Angeles.

Fans of television shows such as *CSI*, *Law and Order*, and *Castle*, among others, will get a kick out of their own, personal body bag or chalk-outline welcome mat. If visitors are disturbed by the gruesome humor in the products, then they will appreciate the reasoning behind opening such a store. The shop exists to "promote how fragile life is and create awareness and responsibility toward one's actions." This marketing and public awareness campaign by the Los Angeles County Coroner has received recognition nation-wide and can be appreciated with such products like the authentic toe tag card, urging readers to not drink and drive.

Third Street Promenade

Santa Monica, California 90401
http://www.downtownsm.com/

This outdoors, pedestrian-only, three blocks-long shopping district hosts many boutiques and restaurants, among other shops. Located in downtown Santa Monica, it is a favorite among regular visitors and locals. The Third Street Promenade will offer many options throughout many price ranges. It hosts weekly farmers markets, while street performers are seen daily. Furthermore, the Promenade is close to other valuable spots, like Santa Monica Place.

The SummerTASTE Wine Tasting Series is held annually for two months between August and October. There are numerous restaurants, bars, and cafés along the Third Street Promenade, so check the website before you go to see whether there are local happy hours or specials being held. Although there are many chain stores and restaurants located along the Promenade, there are some boutiques and local art galleries nestled between the larger stores. Great deals can be found while killing time between the beaches and viewing one of the many live entertainment options Santa Monica offers.

Pacific Coast Highway

This long stretch of sun-kissed Californian roadway is one of the most famous in the world. Featured in movies, television and millions of photographs, the Pacific Coast Highway (PCH), also known as California State Route 1, is the United States west coast ride of a lifetime.

If your vacation plans include California, take the time to drive the 8-hour route along the PCH from Los Angeles to the area approaching Silicon Valley (San Jose area) and San Francisco.

The Pacific Coast Highway links Northern and Southern California across an incredibly scenic, coastal area. Vacationers are able to experience lovely beaches, mountains and delightful small towns on the drive.

Heading from the southern California city of Santa Barbara to Solvang and then on to San Luis Obispo, Big Sur and the northern cities of Carmel and Monterey, the Pacific Coast Highway has many days of activities for leisurely drivers to take in. Whether it is an old mission you want to see or to spend a day in beautiful artistic communities such as Santa Barbara, the Pacific Coast Highway offers activities for every kind of traveler. In fact, with so many fun and unique activities to pick from, it may be challenging to narrow down your fun each day.

If you want to steer clear of the tourists, head into the mountains of Big Sur. If you are seeking a look at the glamour along the coast, visit Carmel-by-the-Sea (where Clint Eastwood has his ranch and was once the mayor) and Monterey to see how celebrities (and golfers) vacation. Those vacationers seeking a European flavor will find Danish culture alive and well in Solvang. Food, gift shops and museums focused on Danish heritage are found throughout this area. Vacationers will find many old missions full of history and cultural heritage. Both Spanish and Native American influences and culture are prevalent in the old missions along the coast. Take the time to visit them as well as the churches and peaceful gardens as you rejuvenate on your relaxing driving vacation.

Culture

The culture found along the Pacific Coast Highway varies in each town and a seaside feel is present in each of these beachfront communities. Vacationers who enjoy the arts can stop at the museums along the PCH. Spanish and Native American art and history can be found here. Local art is found all along the highway where the local artisans find continual inspiration in the mountains and on the seashore.

Great food choices also await vacationers with meals inspired from all over the world. From the Danish foods of Solvang to the Mexican foods found everywhere along the coast, the food of the California coast is delicious. Along the Central Coast, vacationers can find a mix of nature and scenery. From swimsuits to raincoats flip-flops to hiking boots, the PCH has activities to accommodate all moods. Decide how you will spend your time along the coast. Let your interests and explorative side lead the way.

Location & Orientation

The Pacific Coast Highway is located on the west coast of California. It runs the length of the state allowing travelers to see the variety of scenery California has to offer. The Central Coast area is blessed with a mild climate and a blend between city and country living. The PCH takes travelers along the beach, through the mountains and along the Los Padres National Forest. Through seaside bustling towns to quaint villages tucked away from it all, the PCH has so many escapes in store for travelers.

Climate & When to Visit

The climate along the Pacific Coast Highway is beautiful all year round. From sunny days to cool breezy nights, the PCH offers great mild weather for vacationers no matter when you visit. The further north you drive, the foggier the conditions can be. The mountains and forests also provide a different climate as you venture into them. Be prepared for sun, sand, surf and style as you vacation along California's Pacific Coast Highway.

Check out www.pchweather.com or www.visitcalifornia.com/Travel-Tools/Weather/ for the latest weather information along the Pacific Coast Highway.

Sightseeing Highlights

Santa Barbara

Old Mission Santa Barbara

2201 Laguna Street, Santa Barbara, California 93105
Phone: (805) 682-4713
www.santabarbaramission.org

Looking for a vacation with a mission? Visit the Old Mission Santa Barbara. This mission is the first place to visit for those travelers seeking a mix of history and culture. In addition to a church, gift shop and museum, the Mission boasts many acres of magnificent gardens and an array of Native American artifacts.

Self-guided and docent-guided tours are available for those vacationers wanting to learn more about the historic Old Mission Santa Barbara. Tour times average about 30 minutes. During these tours, you are able to see the church and museum, the garden and cemetery. Additional detailed tours are available with reservations for groups. For those visitors interested in learning more about the design and building of the Old Mission Santa Barbara, the Art & Architecture tour provides over an hour of this artistic information. Visitors wishing to spend more time in the garden can reserve a spot on the La Huerta Historic Garden tour. Combination tour packages are also available for interested vacationers. Depending on your available schedule and interests, you can spend an hour or a day at the Old Mission Santa Barbara.

The admission fee for self-guided tours is $5.00 for adults (ages 16 - 64); $4.00 for seniors (over age 65); $1.00 for youth (ages 5 - 15); and children under the age of 4 are admitted for free. The admission fee for docent-guided tours to the public is $8.00 for adults (ages 16 - 64); $7.00 for seniors (over age 65); $4.00 for youth (ages 5 - 15); and children under the age of 4 are admitted for free.

Karpeles Manuscript Library Museum

21 West Anapamu Street, Santa Barbara, California 93101
Phone: (805) 962-5322
www.rain.org/%7Ekarpeles/

Along the Pacific Coast Highway exists one of the rarest museums in the world.

The Karpeles Manuscript Library Museum is full of the most rare documents in history. View famous speeches, various genres of literature and numerous documents written about the cultural and historical issues of our nation and the world. The Museum is open Wednesday through Sunday from 10:00 a.m. to 4:00 p.m., and there is no fee for admission. The museum is closed on Monday and Tuesday and on major U.S. holidays.

Rattlesnake Canyon

Los Padres National Forest
3505 Paradise Road
Santa Barbara, California 93105
Phone: (805) 967-3481
www.go-california.com/Rattlesnake-Canyon-Trail
www.santabarbarahikes.com/hikes/frontcountry/rattlesnake.shtml

If you are a traveler seeking a first-hand look at nature, you can find just what you are looking for at Rattlesnake Canyon. Grab a water bottle and get ready for a backpack journey into California's Rattlesnake Canyon. From the cliffs and rocks to the trails, this Canyon has a wealth of nature to behold. Put on your hiking boots and prepare for an adventure through a Wonderland of Rocks found in the Joshua Tree National Park.

For the vacationer looking to get in touch with nature, camping and picnic areas are available to stop for lunch or an overnight stay along California's Pacific Coast Highway. Located in the Los Padres National Forest, Rattlesnake Canyon is a backpacking adventure that is sure to please. The trail offers easy to moderate trails with minimal elevations for less experienced hikers.

Chumash Painted Cave State Historic Park

Santa Barbara, California 93105
Phone: (805) 733-3713
www.parks.ca.gov/?page_id=602

Operated by the La Purisimia Mission State Historic Park, the Chumash Painted Cave State Historic Park is full of historic paintings artwork dating back to very early times. Created by the Chumash Native Americans, these painted cave walls provide a realistic look at the first known forms of art, communication and writing in this historic park. Vacationers when venturing into the cave should bring warmer clothing to stay warm while taking in the art forms. Some of the art has been dated back to the 1600s. The park is open from dawn until dusk each day for visitors.

Stearns Wharf

211 Stearns Wharf
Santa Barbara, California 93101
Phone: (805) 962-2526
http://stearnswharf.org/

Looking for a way to spend the day near the water? Head to Stearns Wharf to soak up the sea. Check out the Ty Warner Sea Center while you are on the Wharf. Spend the day visiting the numerous shops and restaurants or stop by for a quick bite while exploring the road and activities of the Pacific Coast Highway. Take a stroll through a number of specialty shops all promising to provide a taste of seafront lifestyle for vacationers.

Since 1872, Stearns Wharf has provided a look at a working wharf. The oldest in California, Stearns Wharf is well known for the food and shopping available along the waterfront. When you arrive, grab fishing supplies and catch your own dinner from the world of fresh fish swimming in the nearby waters.

Santa Barbara Museum of Art

1130 State Street, Santa Barbara, California 93101
Phone: (805) 963-4364
www.sbmuseart.org

The Santa Barbara Museum of Art is a fine collection of contemporary and international art.

With great influences in Asian art, this museum is filled with a variety of works. From American Masterpieces to European Classics, the Santa Barbara Museum of Art provides a look at many key works from both sides of the sea. The museum collection at the Santa Barbara Museum of Art includes antiquities, photography, works on paper and Asian, European, American, Modern, Contemporary, and Provenance art works. Art loving vacationers are sure to find what they are looking for inside the walls of this museum.

The museum is open Tuesday through Sunday from 11:00 a.m. to 5:00 p.m.; the museum is closed on Monday and several major holidays. The admission fee is $10.00 for adults; and for seniors (age 65+) and students the admission fee is $6.00. On Sundays, the admission fee is waived so visitors are able to enjoy the museum for free.

Santa Barbara Zoo

500 Niños Drive, Santa Barbara, California 93103
Phone: (805) 962-5339
www.sbzoo.org/

The Santa Barbara Zoo is a great way to spend an hour or a day when you visit the California coast. Visit the Discovery Pavilion or a number of exhibits throughout the park. The cost for adult admission is $14.00.

Children and seniors over 65 years of age have an admission fee of $10.00, and children under 2 are free. Parking for non-members is $6.00. Spend some time in the Barnyard feeding the animals or check out the Dinosaur show. For those vacationers with small children, the Kallman Family Area has many fun activities to enjoy. No trip to the zoo is complete without a ride on the Santa Barbara Zoo Train.

The admission fee for adults and seniors (age 13+) is $4.50 and children (ages 2 – 12) $4.00. Children under 2 years old are welcome with no admission fee. Parking is available for $6.00 per vehicle.

Solvang & Santa Ynez Valley

Santa Ynez Valley Visitors Association

P.O. Box 315
Solvang, California 93464
Phone: (805) 686-0053
http://visitthesantaynezvalley.com/

Spend a day in the Santa Ynez Valley. Take a hike in the Los Padres National Forest or spend some time in the San Rafael Mountains. For the wine loving vacationer, the Santa Ynez Valley offers many fantastic wine tours and vineyard experiences. Take a Segway tour if you are feeling adventurous. Catch a show at the Solvang Theaterfest. Whatever you choose, there are many great ways to see what Solvang has to offer.

Elverhoj Museum of History & Art

1624 Elverhoj Way
Solvang, California 93463
Phone: (805) 686-1211
http://elverhoj.org/

Interested in learning more about Denmark? Think you can't experience international culture while vacationing on the western coast of California? Think again. When visiting the Elverhoj Museum of History and Art, vacationers are able to take a look at Denmark's heritage.

The museum is open in the afternoon on Wednesday through Sunday. The museum is closed on Monday and Tuesday. While admission is free, a $3.00 donation for visitors over the age of 12 is suggested.

Hans Christian Andersen Museum

1680 Mission Drive, Solvang, California 93463
Phone: (805) 688-2052
www.solvangca.com/museum/h1.htm

Visit the land of fairy tales when you stop by the museum dedicated to Hans Christian Andersen. This quaint museum features several rooms filled with Andersen's works.

Books and sketches come to life throughout this museum as they are displayed in a venue like no other. Each year, the museum celebrates Andersen's birthday with cake for all guests. If you want to be part of the celebration, stop by the museum on April 2.

Solvang Vintage Motorcycle Museum

320 Alisal Road
Solvang, California 93463
Phone: (805) 686-9722
www.motosolvang.com

Vacationers who enjoy life on two wheels should be sure to stop by the Solvang Vintage Motorcycle Museum. Rare and collectible motorcycles are always on display at this museum. From European race bikes to collections of car motorcycles, the Solvang Vintage Motorcycle Museum has a bit of motor history for all visitors.

The museum is open each weekend from 11:00 a.m. to 5:00 p.m.; during the week, appointments can be made. The admission fee is $10 for guests over 10 years of age; children under 10 years of age are admitted at no charge.

Old Mission Santa Ines

1760 Mission Drive
Solvang, California 93463
Phone: (805) 688-4815
www.missionsantaines.org/home.html

Visit one California's many missions as you step into the Old Mission Santa Ines. One of the most scenic missions, this historic church overlooks the Santa Ynez River Valley. Learn about the religious history that surrounds this mission by taking a tour throughout the grounds.

The admission fee for visitors age 11 and over is $5.00. Self-guided tours are available daily from 9:00 a.m. to 4:30 p.m. each day. The mission is closed on major holidays.

San Luis Obispo

San Luis Obispo Convention Bureau

811 El Capitan Way
San Luis Obispo, California 93401
Phone: (805) 781-2777
http://visitslo.com

Sometimes called the "happiest place on earth," San Luis Obispo is a great scenic stop on your Pacific Coast Highway vacation drive.

Music, beaches, hiking, biking and fun can be found each day in this city. If you have like adventure, off road ATV parks are also nearby. Get out and get happy in San Luis Obispo.

Hearst Castle

750 Hearst Castle Road, San Simeon, California 93452
Phone: (800) 444-4445
www.hearstcastle.org

Looking for the royal treatment when on your visit to California? If so, make sure you add a stop at the Hearst Castle to your list of things to do while you are on your vacation. This is where a classic episode of Star Trek was filmed in the 1960's. A tour of this beautiful castle is a not-to-be-missed highlight of a visit to the Pacific Coast Highway. The admission fee for guided tours of Hearst Castle is $35.00 for adults and $12.00 for children.

Big Sur

Big Sur Chamber of Commerce
P.O. Box 87
Big Sur, California 93920
Phone: (831) 667-2100
www.bigsurcalifornia.org

Some vacationers are looking for a place to truly escape the fast-pace of daily life. Big Sur is this destination. Here, visitors will find scenery that compares to no place else. Visitors can enjoy the highway drives, mountain hikes and have a fantastic vacation without crowds or busy schedules. Savor the moments that Big Sur can provide.

Bixby Bridge

N 36.371° W 121.900, Route 1, Big Sur Highway
Monterey, California
http://byways.org/explore/byways/2301/places/11760/

Seen in numerous commercials and movies, Big Sur's Bixby Bridge is one of the most recognizable structures in the United States. Finished in the 1930s, Bixby Bridge is a top tourist destination for vacationers visiting the west coast of California. Whether in a movie or on film, this highly photographed bridge is a common sight in the world of media. Take this opportunity to have your own moments captured along Bixby Bridge.

Carmel

Point Lobos State Reserve Park

Route 1, Box 62, Carmel, California
Phone: (866) 338-7227
www.pointlobos.org

Nature-loving travelers will find a day at Point Lobos State Reserve Park a great way to spend the day along the Pacific Coast Highway.

Home to hundreds of animals, birds and plants, Point Lobos is a scenic nature reserve. The beauty found throughout this area is protected so it is available for future generations. Spend time checking out the wildlife and taking in the scenery. Vacationers with a love for photography will find Point Lobos a great place to take in the sights and take some snapshots.

Carmel Chamber of Commerce
Carmel, California 93921
Phone: (831) 624-2522
www.carmelcalifornia.com

Vacationers flock to Carmel-by-the-Sea when they visit the west coast of California. Carmel is a place to enjoy a small artistic community with some fantastic craft shops and art galleries. Music lovers can enjoy nightly shows. Food lovers can seek many local flavors. And, shoppers can find plenty of places to search for the next great buy. If your vacation plans include the beach or hiking, Carmel will also provide you the activities you are looking for. Combine your trip to Carmel with a visit to nearby Monterey and the 17-Mile Drive.

San Carlos Borromeo de Carmelo Mission

3080 Rio Road, Carmel, California
Phone: (831) 624-1271
www.carmelmission.org/museum

In California, visitors will discover a world of Missions including the San Carlos Borromeo de Carmelo Mission in Carmel. Discover the spiritual heritage found in this historic location. Visit the Basilica Church and the five museums with interesting artifacts on display.

The admission fee for adults is $6.50; seniors $4.00 and children $2.00 (ages 7 and over). For children under the age of six, admission is free. The Mission is open every day of the week but closed on Easter, Thanksgiving and Christmas.

Monterey

Cannery Row

Cannery Row & Recreation Trail, Monterey, California
www.canneryrow.com

Take a walk on Ocean View Drive when you visit Cannery Row in Monterey.

This street was memorialized in the work of author John Steinbeck in his book, Cannery Row. Visit this bustling location for a wonderful dining experience, fun with the family or a night on the town.

Monterey Bay Aquarium

886 Cannery Row
Monterey, California 93940
Phone: (831) 648-4800
www.montereybayaquarium.org

A stop at the Monterey Bay Aquarium will bring the sea to life as you visit the exhibits and nature waiting for you around each corner. Learn about the plants and animals including jellyfish, whales and sharks. Witness feeding time with the sea life as well. The hours of operations are 10:00 a.m. to 5:00 p.m. each day.

Admission to the Aquarium is $34.95 for adult guests and $21.95 for children (ages 3 – 12). There is no admission fee for children under the age of 3. Senior citizens and students can gain admission for $31.95.

Pebble Beach Golf Links

The Lodge at Pebble Beach
1700 17-Mile Drive, Pebble Beach, California 93953
Phone: (831) 647-7500
www.pebblebeach.com

The Pebble Beach Golf Links has been the home to the U.S. Open Tournament five times. For golf-lovers, a round of golf on this course will be a memory to last a lifetime. Those hoping to run into a professional golfer or celebrity will have a good chance when visiting this golf course and the Pebble Beach Lodge. After a round of golf, take a beautiful trip along the nearby 17-Mile Drive.

17-Mile Drive

Pebble Beach, California 93953
Phone: (800) 654-9300
www.pebblebeach.com

The 17-Mile Drive is a highly recommended (and low-cost) way to spend time in the Pebble Beach area of California. This roadway is beautiful and is a famous Californian landmark. The road begins at Pacific Grove and concludes at Pebble Beach. Along the way, drivers should stop at Stillwater Cove or head to the end of the drive for a round of golf at Pebble Beach Golf Links.

Recommendations for the Budget Traveler

Places to Stay

Santa Barbara

Hotel Oceana Santa Barbara

202 West Cabrillo Boulevard, Santa Barbara, California 93101
Phone: (805) 965-4577
www.hoteloceanasantabarbara.com

Charm, convenience and beauty await vacationers who check into the Hotel Oceana.

Soak up the sun in the courtyard or take in the views that surround you. Guests can enjoy the health club, pools and Jacuzzi or walk to nearby shopping. Room rates start at $119 per night.

Inn at East Beach

1029 Orilla Del Mar
Santa Barbara, California 93101
Phone: (805) 965-0546
www.innateastbeach.com

Looking for a hotel that is close to the beach? Inn at East Beach has just what you need. A short walk to the beach and an economical rate make this an excellent choice for your lodging needs in Santa Barbara. Room rates average $100 per night. Some rooms have king beds and kitchenettes available.

Solvang

Wine Valley Inn

1564 Copenhagen Drive, Solvang, California 93463
Phone: (800) 824-6444
www.winevalleyinn.com

Located in the heart of a wine-lover's paradise is the Wine Valley Inn.

This Inn provides luxury accommodations at a moderate lodging rate. Gardens, fireplaces, Jacuzzis and private decks add romance and charm to this Inn. Cottages rooms provide kitchenettes and room for vacationing groups of 4 – 6 people. Rates range from $104 to $195 a night.

King Frederik Inn

1617 Copenhagen Drive
Solvang, California 93463
Phone: (800) 549-9955
www.kingfrederikinn.com

Take your Danish experience in Solvang to the next level by staying a night or two at the King Frederick Inn. Guests enjoy free Wi-Fi and a continental breakfast each day. A heated pool provides an opportunity for vacationers to get in some exercise while traveling and the hot tub offers a chance for relaxation. Room rates range from $89 to $129 per night.

San Luis Obispo

Vagabond Inn, San Luis Obispo

210 Madonna Road
San Luis Obispo, California 93405
Phone: (805) 544-4710
www.vagabondinnsanluisobispo.com

Traveling like a vagabond? The Vagabond Inn San Luis Obispo has the lodging you seek. Located bear the Pacific Coast Highway, this hotel provides travelers with a chance to get off the road and take a rest. A pool and spa are available for vacationers to enjoy daily along with a continental breakfast. Room rates range from $65 to $89 per night depending on the nights of stay and the time of year.

La Cuesta Inn

2407 Monterey Street, San Luis Obispo, California 93401
Phone: (800) 543-2777
www.lacuestainn.com

Looking for a hotel for your next vacation? Traveling on business? La Cuesta Inn has just what you need for either setting. Enjoy wine tasting at the local wineries, a day at the beach or a mountain drive adventure – the choice is yours. Room rates range from $89 for a standard room to $239 per night for the king executive suite.

Big Sur

Ripplewood Resort

47047 Highway 1
Big Sur, California 93920
Phone: (831) 667-2242
www.ripplewoodresort.com

Ripplewood Resort has something different in store for visitors. Cabins on the river provide a true Big Sur retreat experience. The Ripplewood Resort opened in the 1920s to provide vacationers with an up close look at the beauty of Big Sur. Many of the cabins include fireplaces, skylights, decks and kitchens, but features vary depending on the cabin you reserve. Cabin rates start at $95 per night.

Davenport Roadhouse

31 Davenport Avenue, Davenport, California 95017
Phone: (831) 426-8801
www.davenportroadhouse.com

The Davenport Roadhouse offers travelers an opportunity to stay in Big Sur in a location that is far off of the well-beaten vacationer's path. With a restaurant and store, this hotel provides you all the convenience you need while allowing you to take a stop off of the Pacific Coast Highway for the night. Room rates start at $120 per night.

Carmel

Carmel Mission Inn

3665 Rio Road
Carmel, California 93923
Phone: (800) 348-9090
www.carmelmissioninn.com

Venturing to Carmel or the Monterey Peninsula can be costly, but the Carmel Mission Inn provides an alternative to other pricey options. Spend your time relaxing on the beach or golfing – the Carmel Mission Inn is close to either activity. In the hotel, a heated pool, spa, gym and free Wi-Fi await guests. Free parking allows travelers to spend vacation money on the fun things in Carmel. Room rates start at around $160 per night. For romance or business, the Carmel Mission Inn has just what you are looking for on your getaway.

Carmel River Inn

26600 Oliver Road, Carmel, California 93923
Phone: (831) 624-1575
www.carmelriverinn.com

The Carmel River Inn is an excellent lodging choice for vacationers in search of a charming hotel for their stay.

This lovely Inn is located just outside Carmel-by-the-Sea, which allows vacationers to get away from the crowds when traveling. The nearby river provides a calm setting for guests to enjoy as they venture through the gardens and surrounding meadows. Room rates start at $80 per night and many Internet specials are available for those travelers hoping to save some travel dollars.

Monterey

Cannery Row Inn

200 Foam Street
Monterey, California 93940
Phone: (831) 375-2411
http://canneryrowinn.com

Guests here enjoy the convenience of a walking to Monterey's activities. Visit Fisherman's Wharf or the Monterey Bay Aquarium, which are just minutes away. Free Wi-Fi adds to the conveniences available to travelers. Balconies and patios in each room help guests get a great view of the beautiful scenery. Room rates at Cannery Row Inn start at $72.00 per night.

Casa Munras

700 Munras Avenue
Monterey, California 93940
Phone: (831) 375-2411
www.hotelcasamunras.com

Feel the Spanish culture alive at Casa Munras. The charm of the Spanish style hotel expands outdoors to the courtyard. The hotel is located in close proximity to many of Monterey's activities or stay back to spend a day at the hotel spa. Guess can enjoy a pool, health club, and free Wi-Fi. Room rates start at $132.00 per night.

Places to Eat

Santa Barbara

The Brewhouse Santa Barbara

229 West Montecito Street, Santa Barbara, California
Phone: (805) 884-4664
www.brewhousesb.com

Handcrafted beers are on tap at The Brewhouse Santa Barbara. The menu features affordable dining options for all vacationers. On the weekends, the Brewhouse offers a brunch buffet that is sure to please.

Taqueria El Bajio

129 North Milpas Street
Santa Barbara, California
Phone: (805) 884-1828

Amazing food at an affordable price - that is what you will find at Taqueria El Bajio. Healthy portions make your dollar go even further when traveling through Santa Barbara. The fabulous flavors only add to your experience.

Solvang

Belgian Café

1671 Copenhagen Drive
Solvang, California 93463
Phone: (805) 688-6630

The Belgian Café offers vacationers a European experience in the middle of Solvang, California. From French toast to fresh soups, guests have a variety of food choices. Be sure to get an order of their famous crepes and Belgian waffles.

Viking Garden Restaurant

446-C Alisal Road
Solvang, California 93463
Phone: (805) 693-4354
www.solvangdanishcuisine.com

When in Solvang it is important to experience the culture that exists at every turn. The Viking Garden Restaurant offers a nice blend of Danish and German food while providing American and Mexican food options, too. What a great combination for all types of vacationers. Great prices only add to the great dining experience.

San Luis Obispo

Franks Famous Hot Dogs

950 California Boulevard
San Luis Obispo, California
Phone: (805) 541-3488
www.franksfamoushotdog.com

Looking for some lunch and some history, head over to Franks Famous Hot Dogs. This hot dog shop is open each day from 6:30 a.m. to 9:00 p.m. and they stay pretty busy. Call ahead to have your order ready to go.

Chino's Rock & Tacos

98 Niblick Road
San Luis Obispo, California 93446
Phone: (805) 226-2926
www.chinosrocks.com

This restaurant provides visitors with a unique Mexican food experience. Chino's Roc & Tacos offers great food, great music and best of all great prices to those who stop by. The best part of this restaurant is the concern for the community and people by utilizing "green" technologies and providing donations to local organizations.

Big Sur

Nepenthe Restaurant

48510 Highway One
Big Sur, California 93920
Phone: (831) 667-2345
www.nepenthebigsur.com

Enjoy lunch and a bit of history when you stop for a bite at the Nepenthe Restaurant in Big Sur. This restaurant is open daily for lunch from 11:30 a.m. to 4:30 p.m. every day. They are also open for dinner from 5:00 – 10:00 p.m. expect on Thanksgiving and Christmas. Visit the Phoenix Shop to purchase some souvenirs from your trip.

Rocky Point Restaurant

36700 Highway 1
Big Sur, California
Phone: (831) 624-2933
www.rocky-point.com

Looking for a meal with a view? The Rocky Point Restaurant offers the meal and view you are seeking. This restaurant is located along the Pacific Coast Highway in Big Sur and offers guests a view of the spectacular scenery. The restaurant is open for breakfast, lunch and dinner each day. An early bird dinner special allows guests to enjoy a four-course dinner for a discounted price.

Carmel

Bahama Island Steakhouse

3690 The Barnyard
Carmel-By-The-Sea, California 93923
Phone: (831) 626-0430
http://bahamaislandsteakhouse.com

An affordable steakhouse awaits you at Bahama Island. Enjoy the heated outdoor patio all year long or stay warm by the fireplace. Whatever you choose, Bahama Island provides a great tropical atmosphere and delicious food.

Earthbound Farm

7250 Carmel Valley Road
Carmel, California
Phone: (831) 625-6219
www.ebfarm.com

Some vacationers are searching for the freshness that only California has to offer. For those folks, Earthbound Farm is waiting to take you on a food journey. Earthbound Farm is an organic restaurant that offers a wide variety of delicious food selections. The outdoor dining experience only adds to the freshness of the food.

Monterey

Sly McFly's

700 A Cannery Row
Monterey, California 93940
Phone: (831) 649-8050
www.slymcflys.net

A racing restaurant with a story is what you will find at Sly McFly's. Located in the heart of Cannery Row, this restaurant provides great food and great blues music.

Papa Chevo's Taco Shop

229 Cannery Row
Monterey, California 93940
Phone: (831) 372-7298
www.papachevos.com

If you are hungry and on a budget, head to Papa Chevo's Taco Shop. Serving food all day long, you can always find an affordable meal at Papa Chevo's. This restaurant is a popular stop for many travelers in Monterey.

Places to Shop

Santa Barbara

Santa Barbara Farmer's Market

232 Anacapa Street
Santa Barbara, California 93101
Phone: (805) 962-5354
www.sbfarmersmarket.org

Even the vacationer can enjoy a day at the famer's market. Freshness comes alive at Santa Barbara's Farmer's Market. Stop by to get local homegrown favorites to take on your Pacific Coast Highway adventure.

Paseo Nuevo Shopping Center

State & De La Guerra Streets
Santa Barbara, California 93101
Phone: (805) 963-7147
www.paseonuevoshopping.com

Ready for a retail extravaganza? Paseo Nuevo provides a great shopping experience for all sorts of vacationers. Restaurants, shops and retailers line the Paseo Nuevo Shopping Center. Fashion is waiting for you at Paseo Nuevo!

Solvang & Santa Ynez Valley

Ingeborg's

1679 Copenhagen Drive
Solvang, California 93463
Phone: (805) 688-5612
www.ingeborgs.com

For over 50 years, Ingeborg's of Solvang has been creating delicious chocolates. This Danish Chocolate shop allows vacationers to bring the taste of Danish chocolate home.

Windmill Glassworks

436A Alisal Road
Solvang, California 93463
Phone: (805) 688-8722
http://windmillglassworks.com

This gift shop brings Danish life to life. Offering unique gifts for every traveler, visitors are sure to find what they are looking for. Located in the heart of Solvang, this gift shop provides great gifts at a great price.

San Luis Obispo

Apple Farm Gift Shop & Millhouse

2015 Monterey Street
San Luis Obispo, California 93401
Phone: (805) 541-0369
www.applefarm.com

Find a unique blend of charm and trend when you visit the Apple Farm. This gift shop provides shoppers with an opportunity to visit a working millhouse or grab a sweet in the bakery. An outlet center provides gifts for the budget vacationer.

Kwirkworld

766 Higuera Street
San Luis Obispo, California 93401
Phone: (805) 544-4222
www.kwikworld.com

Shoppers who sway from normal should stop by Kwirkworld. This unique gift shop provides fun and "quirky" way to bring home great souvenirs and a bit of crazy California.

Big Sur

Local Color

46840 Highway One, Suite 6
Big Sur, California 93920
Phone: (831) 667-0481
www.bigsurlocalcolor.com

Searching for Californian treasure? For those shoppers who want to buy local art, Local Color features the work of hundreds of Californian artists. Gifts include paintings jewelry and other art works.

Big Sur Bizarre

47520 Highway One
Big Sur, California 93920
Phone: (831) 667-0446
www.bigsurdeli.com

Shopping on an empty stomach can be dangerous! The owners of the Big Sur Bizarre have taken care of this problem. Vacationers stopping here are able to grab lunch at the Big Sur Deli and shop for souvenirs at the gift shop. One-stop shopping. For those travelers who are camping, the Big Sur Bizarre offers camping supplies and groceries, too.

Carmel

Carmel Bay Company

Corner of Ocean Avenue & Lincoln
Carmel-by-the-Sea, California 93921
Phone: (831) 624-3868
http://carmelbaycompany.com

For those vacationers searching for a piece of California to bring home, the Carmel Bay Company offers a unique opportunity. In this shop, shoppers are able to purchase works from local artisans. The shop is open daily from 10:00 a.m. until 5:00 p.m.; the shop is closed on Thanksgiving and Christmas.

The Barnyard Shopping Village

3618 The Barnyard
Carmel, California 93923
Phone: (831) 624-8886
www.thebarnyard.com

Since the 1970s, this shopping location has been a stop for many California visitors. Vacationers can visit local shops, galleries or relax and enjoy the beautiful charm of the gardens and courtyard that surround The Barnyard Shopping Village. Spend the day spending money as you mill around the barnyard of shopping.

Monterey

Ghirardelli Chocolate & Ice Cream Shop

600 Cannery Row, Monterey, California 93940
Phone: (831) 373-0997
www.ghirardelli.com

Bring home a taste of California when you stop by the Ghirardelli Chocolate Company's Monterey Shop.

With the home of Ghirardelli being located in nearby San Francisco, these chocolates are a staple for vacationers visiting the coast. Made with the best ingredients, these premium chocolates are a favorite of many visitors. The Ghirardelli Chocolate & Ice Cream Shop in Monterey provides a taste of these delightful goodies for all visitors looking for a treat to please their sweet tooth.

The Wharf's General Store

14 Fisherman's Wharf
Monterey, California 93940
Phone: (831) 649-4404
www.twgs.com

The Wharf's General Store is full of gifts, souvenirs and all the fun stuff travelers seek for those friends and family who didn't come along on the trip. Visit this huge gift shop in the heart of Monterey on Fisherman's Wharf.

Printed in Germany
by Amazon Distribution
GmbH, Leipzig